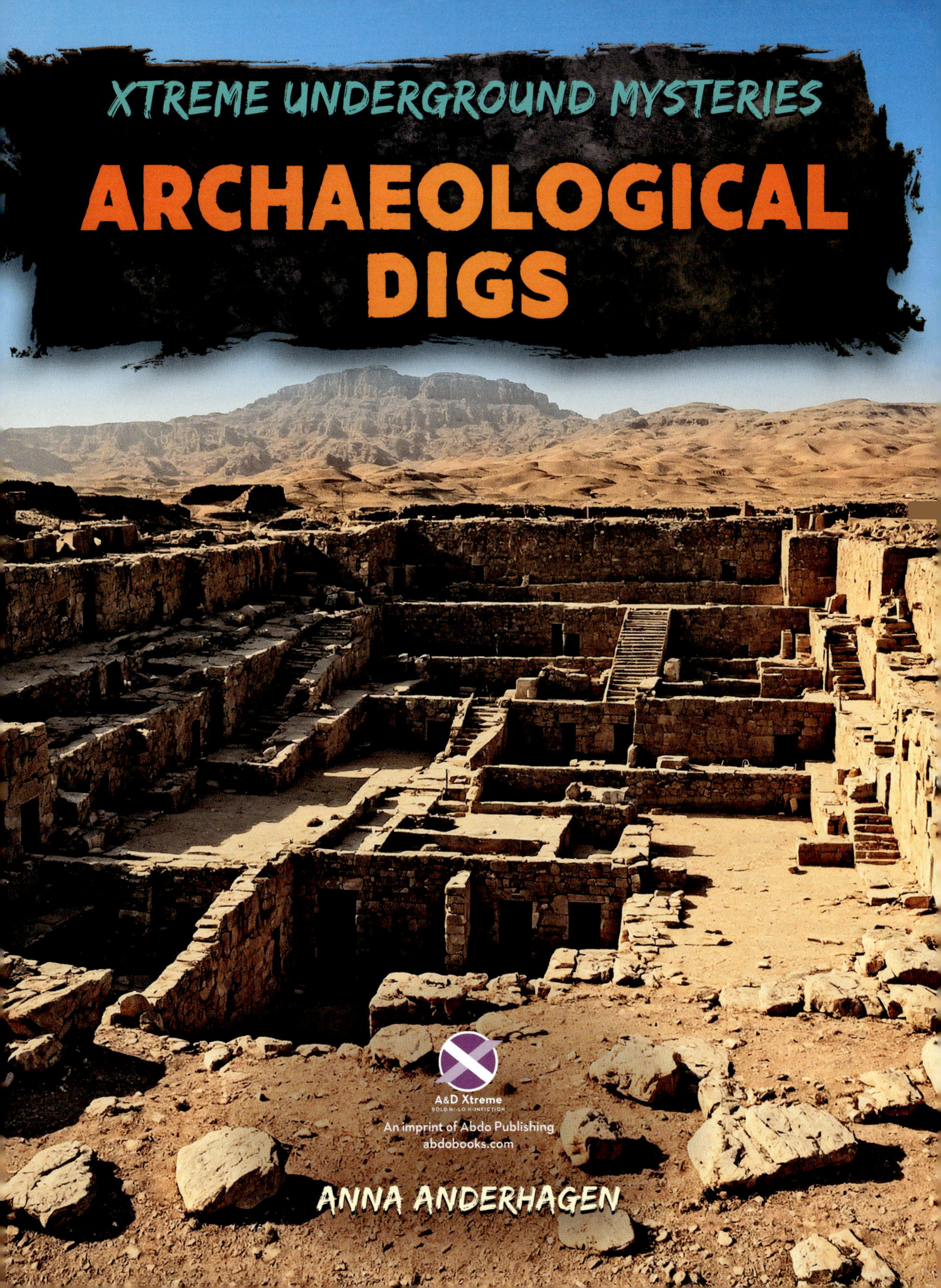
XTREME UNDERGROUND MYSTERIES
ARCHAEOLOGICAL DIGS
A&D Xtreme
An imprint of Abdo Publishing
abdobooks.com
ANNA ANDERHAGEN

# TAKE IT TO THE XTREME!

GET READY FOR AN EXTREME ADVENTURE!
THE PAGES OF THIS BOOK WILL TAKE YOU INTO
THE WONDROUS WORLD BENEATH YOUR FEET.
WHEN YOU HAVE FINISHED READING THIS BOOK, TAKE THE
XTREME CHALLENGE ON PAGE 45 ABOUT WHAT YOU'VE LEARNED!

**ABDOBOOKS.COM**
Published by Abdo Publishing, a division of ABDO, PO Box 398166, Minneapolis, Minnesota 55439.

Printed in the United States of America, North Mankato, MN.
102025
012026

Design: Kelly Doudna, Mighty Media, Inc.
Production: Mighty Media, Inc.
Editor: Katherine Chu

Cover Photograph: Naeemphotographer2/Shutterstock
Interior Photographs: Alfredo Cerra/Shutterstock, pp. 24–25; ATSZ56/Wikimedia Commons, pp. 26–27; burnstuff2003/Adobe Stock, p. 44; Dan Gabriel Atanasie/Shutterstock, pp. 20–21; Eric Ewing/Wikimedia Commons, pp. 38–39; FrentaN/Shutterstock, pp. 14–15; Gary Todd/Wikimedia Commons, p. 11 (inset bottom); Hernan Bieler/Shutterstock, pp. 22–23; Jawwad Ali/Shutterstock, p. 11 (inset top); jsnewtonian/Adobe Stock, pp. 36–37; khd/Shutterstock, pp. 16–17; Michael Schneider/Adobe Stock, pp. 32–33; muratart/Shutterstock, pp. 28–29; Naeemphotographer2/Shutterstock, p. 1; Sergey-73/Shutterstock, pp. 4–5; Sezai/Adobe Stock, pp. 6–7; Shozib/Adobe Stock, pp. 8–9, 10–11; Simone Crespiatico/Shutterstock, pp. 18–19; Squier, Ephraim George/Flickr, pp. 40–41; sumikophoto/Shutterstock, pp. 34–35; The Ohio State Museum, Columbus/Columbus Metropolitan Library, pp. 42–43; Thomas Roche/Adobe Stock, pp. 30–31; TripDeeDee Photo/Shutterstock, pp. 12–13
Design Elements: tsayuet/Adobe Stock (rocky texture); Tunatura/Adobe Stock (tunnel texture)

**LIBRARY OF CONGRESS CONTROL NUMBER: 2025939067**
**PUBLISHER'S CATALOGING-IN-PUBLICATION DATA**
Names: Anderhagen, Anna, author.
Title: Archaeological digs / by Anna Anderhagen
Description: Minneapolis, Minnesota : Abdo Publishing, 2026 | Series: Xtreme underground mysteries | Includes online resources and index.
Identifiers: ISBN 9781098297794 (lib. bdg.) | ISBN 9798384930600 (ebook)
Subjects: LCSH: Excavations (Archaeology)--Juvenile literature. | Archaeology--Juvenile literature. | Geosciences--Juvenile literature. | Earth sciences--Juvenile literature.
Classification: DDC 913.08--dc23

# CONTENTS

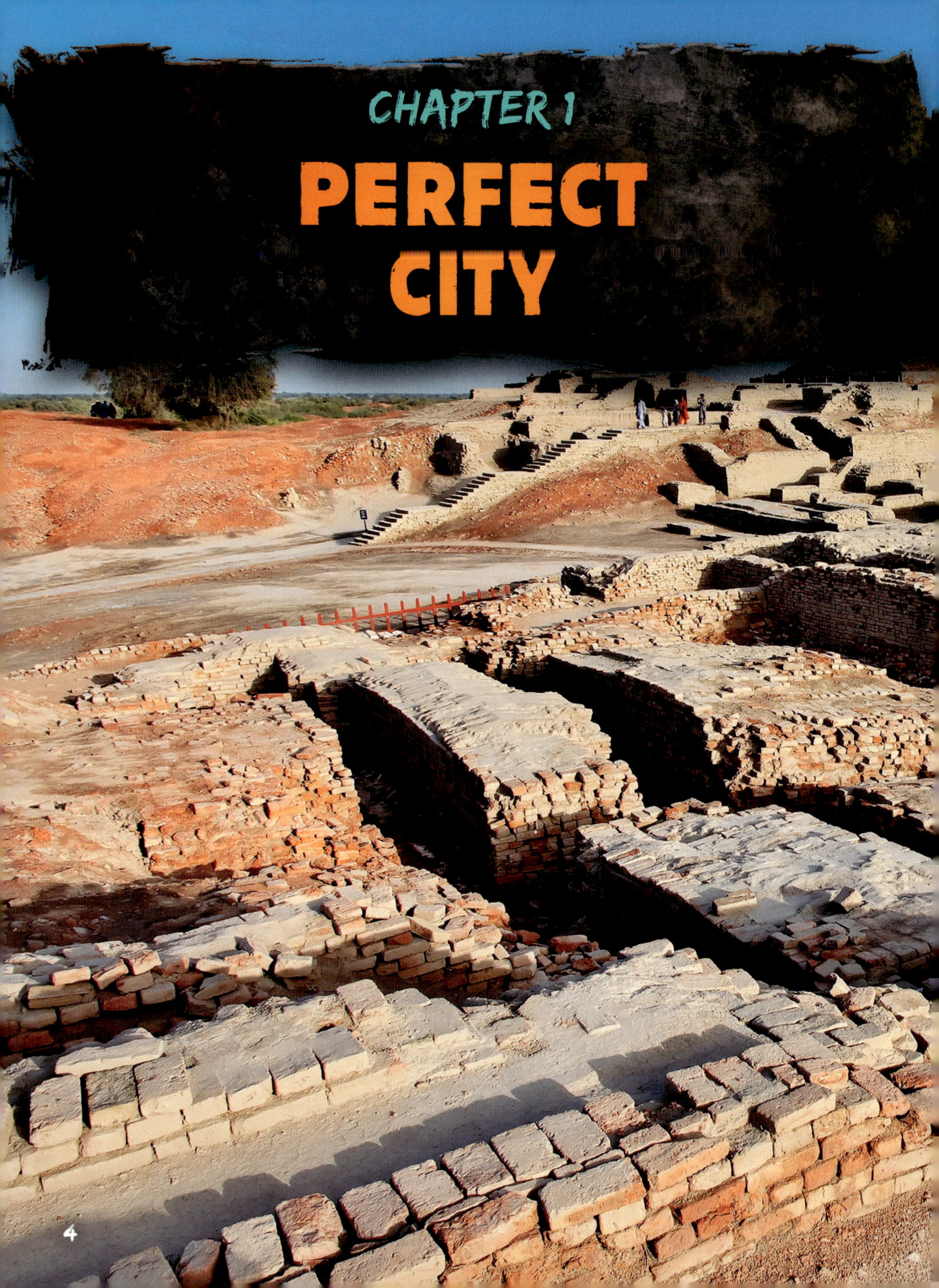

CHAPTER 1

# PERFECT CITY

Archaeologist R. D. Banerji was exploring the Indus River Valley in Pakistan. He heard about a buried site in the area and decided to study it. Banerji began digging and found ancient **artifacts**! He dug deeper and started to uncover an entire city. Banerji had discovered Mohenjo Daro!

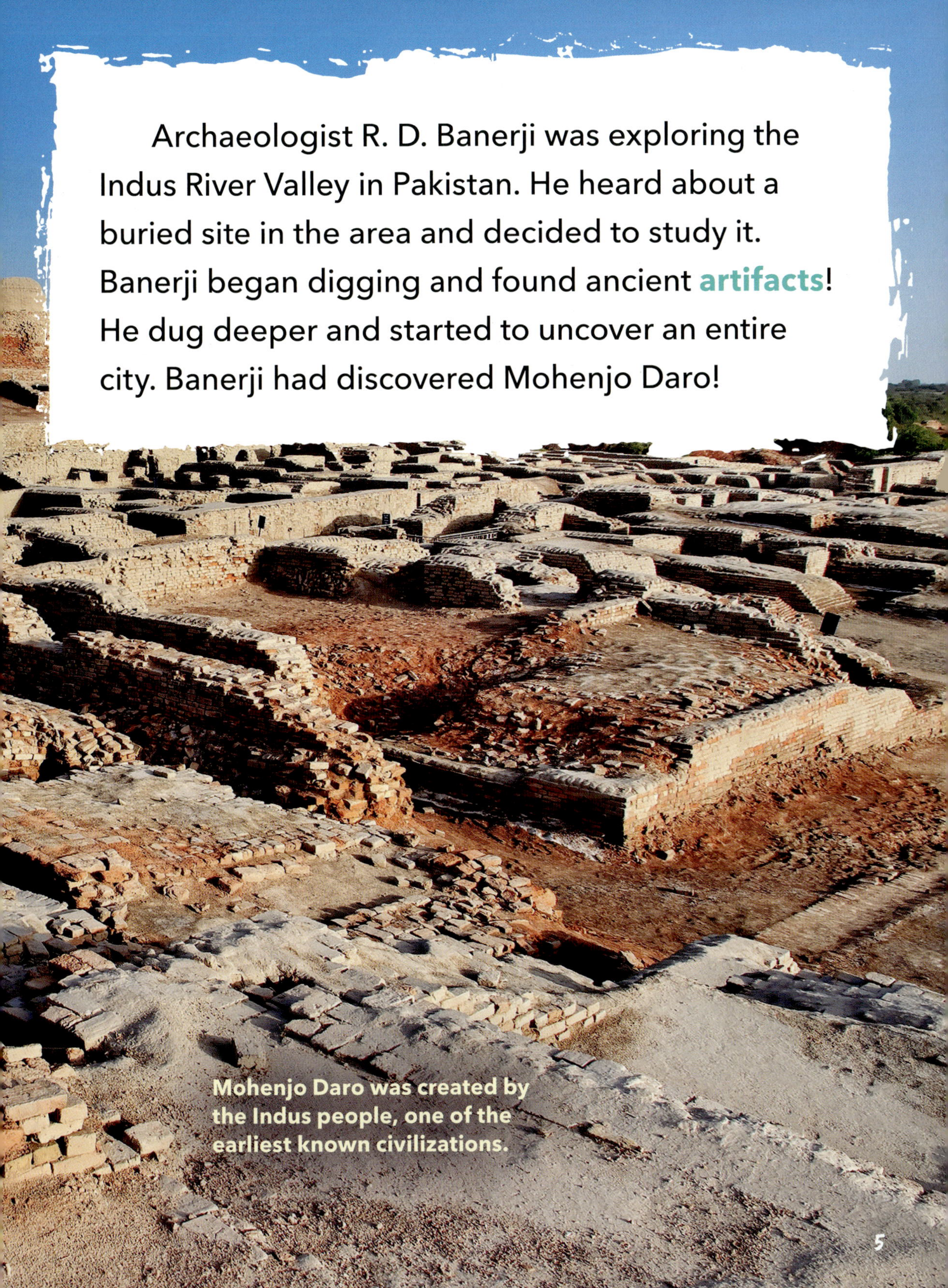

Mohenjo Daro was created by the Indus people, one of the earliest known civilizations.

## CHAPTER 2

# MYSTERIOUS SITES

Archaeologists learn about human history. They do this by studying objects that people leave behind. They explore buried cities, **cenotes**, **effigy mounds**, and more.

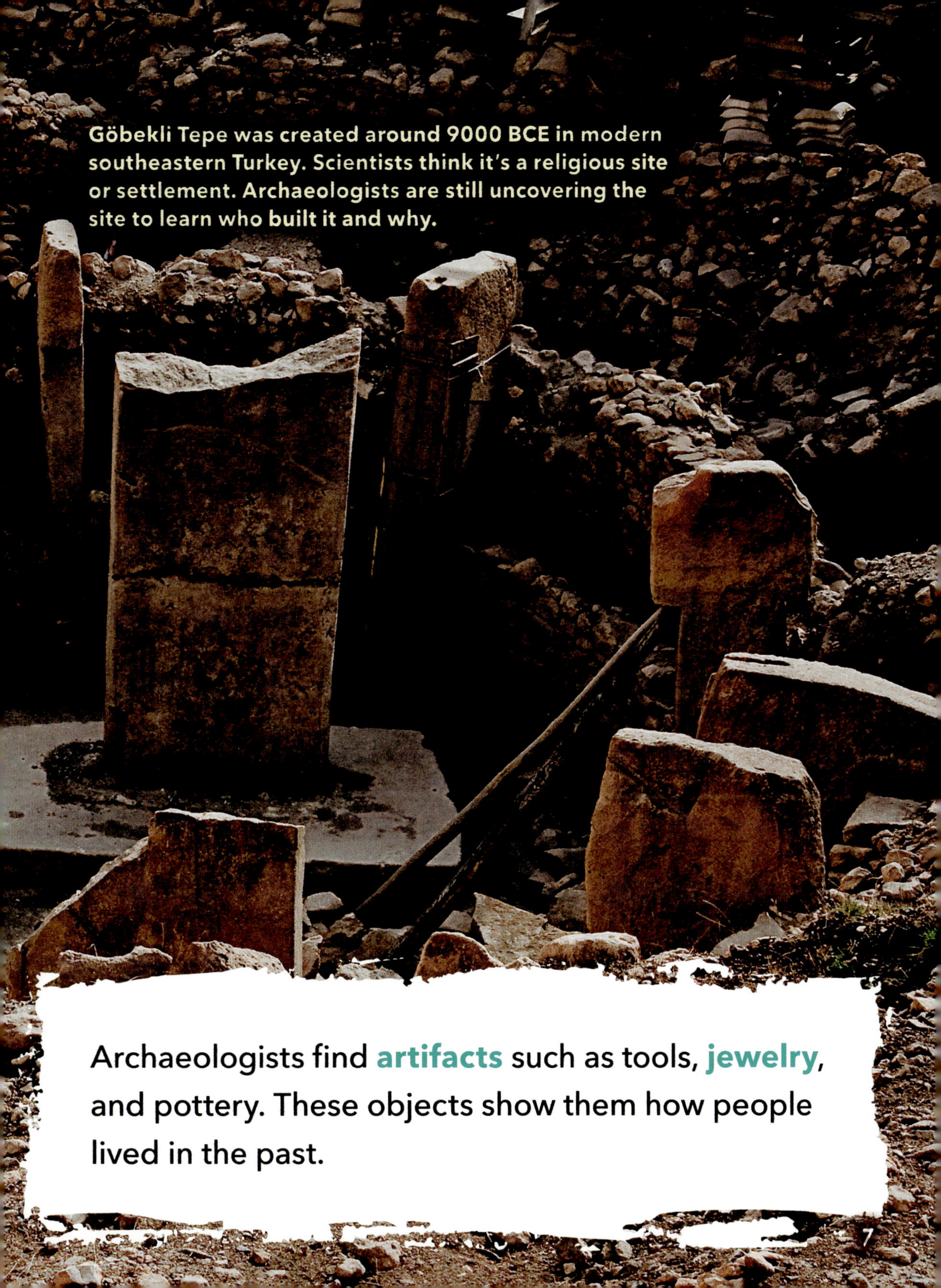

Göbekli Tepe was created around 9000 BCE in modern southeastern Turkey. Scientists think it's a religious site or settlement. Archaeologists are still uncovering the site to learn who built it and why.

Archaeologists find **artifacts** such as tools, **jewelry**, and pottery. These objects show them how people lived in the past.

## CHAPTER 3

# MOHENJO DARO

Mohenjo Daro in modern-day Pakistan was an ancient city from 2500 BCE. It was one of the most advanced cities of its time. Many houses had courtyards, wells, and bathrooms. Clay pipes carried waste to underground sewers. These drained into rivers and helped keep the city clean.

Mohenjo Daro's buildings are laid out like a grid. Archaeologists think this means the city was planned out before it was built.

In 1922, archaeologists began to slowly uncover Mohenjo Daro. They learned how the people there lived long ago. They found drawings and writing on pottery and other objects. They also discovered small statues of people wearing clothes and **jewelry**.

Historians believe around 35,000 people lived and worked in Mohenjo Daro.

## XTREME FACT

Archaeologists studied the Indus River Valley in detail. They found many **artifacts** at different sites. Some artifacts had drawings of unicorns on them!

**Archaeologists are still working to understand what the drawings on the Mohenjo Daro artifacts mean.**

## XTREME FACT

**Scientists are still trying to understand why people left Mohenjo Daro around 1500 BCE.**

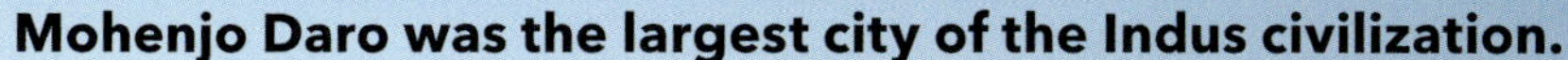

**Mohenjo Daro was the largest city of the Indus civilization.**

Mohenjo Daro is in danger from high heat, flooding, and more. **Historians** warn that the site could be destroyed. So, it needs to be protected and preserved. Archaeologists have asked the **United Nations** to help them do this.

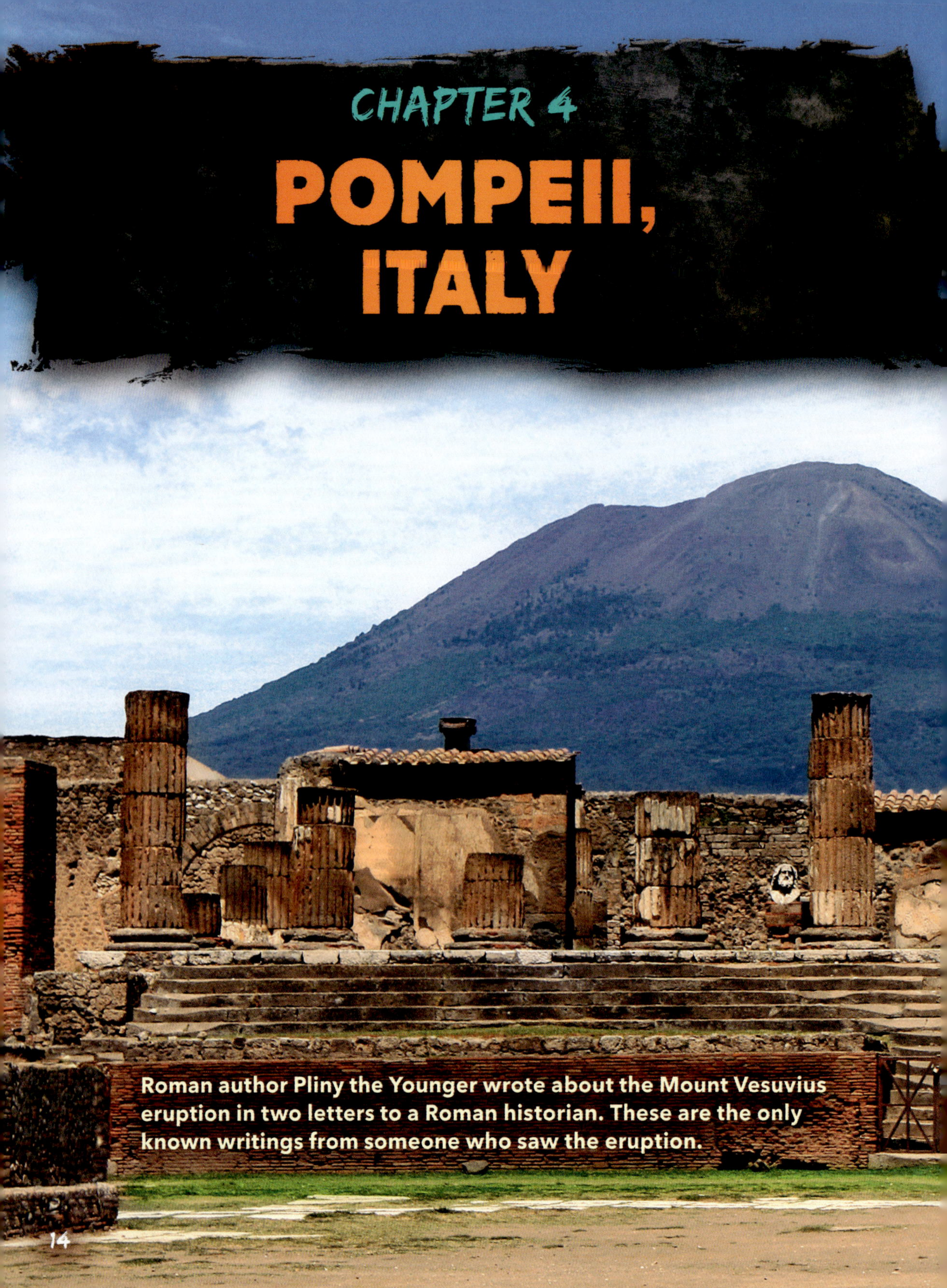

# CHAPTER 4

# POMPEII, ITALY

Roman author Pliny the Younger wrote about the Mount Vesuvius eruption in two letters to a Roman historian. These are the only known writings from someone who saw the eruption.

The city of Pompeii in southern Italy flourished about 2,000 years ago. But then the **volcano** Mount Vesuvius erupted in 79 CE. It blasted smoke, rock, ash, and toxic gas into the air. The volcanic eruption buried the city. It also trapped and killed many of the 12,000 people living there.

The eruption covered Pompeii in layers of ash up to 23 feet (7 m) deep. These layers preserved buildings, artwork, and even the forms of bodies. Most preserved bodies looked like they were taking cover or trying to escape from the eruption.

Archaeologists have found more than 1,000 preserved body forms in Pompeii.

Archaeologists can learn a lot about ancient Roman life from Pompeii. This is because the city was so well preserved. For example, archaeologists have found businesses known as **thermopolia** in Pompeii. These places sold hot food and drinks in large clay jars.

In 2024, archaeologists uncovered an entire city block. It had a laundry, bakery, and huge house. **Historians** think the house belonged to Aulus Rustius Verus, a wealthy politician.

Many thermopolia sold foods such as duck, goat, pig, fish, and snails.

Archaeologists still study Pompeii. They continue to make new discoveries. They also work to preserve the site and its **artifacts**.

## XTREME FACT

More than three million people live by Mount Vesuvius today. Scientists think it's overdue for another big eruption. They closely watch the **volcano's** activity so they can help people leave before it erupts.

Pompeii is also one of Italy's most popular places to visit. About 2.5 million people go to Pompeii every year.

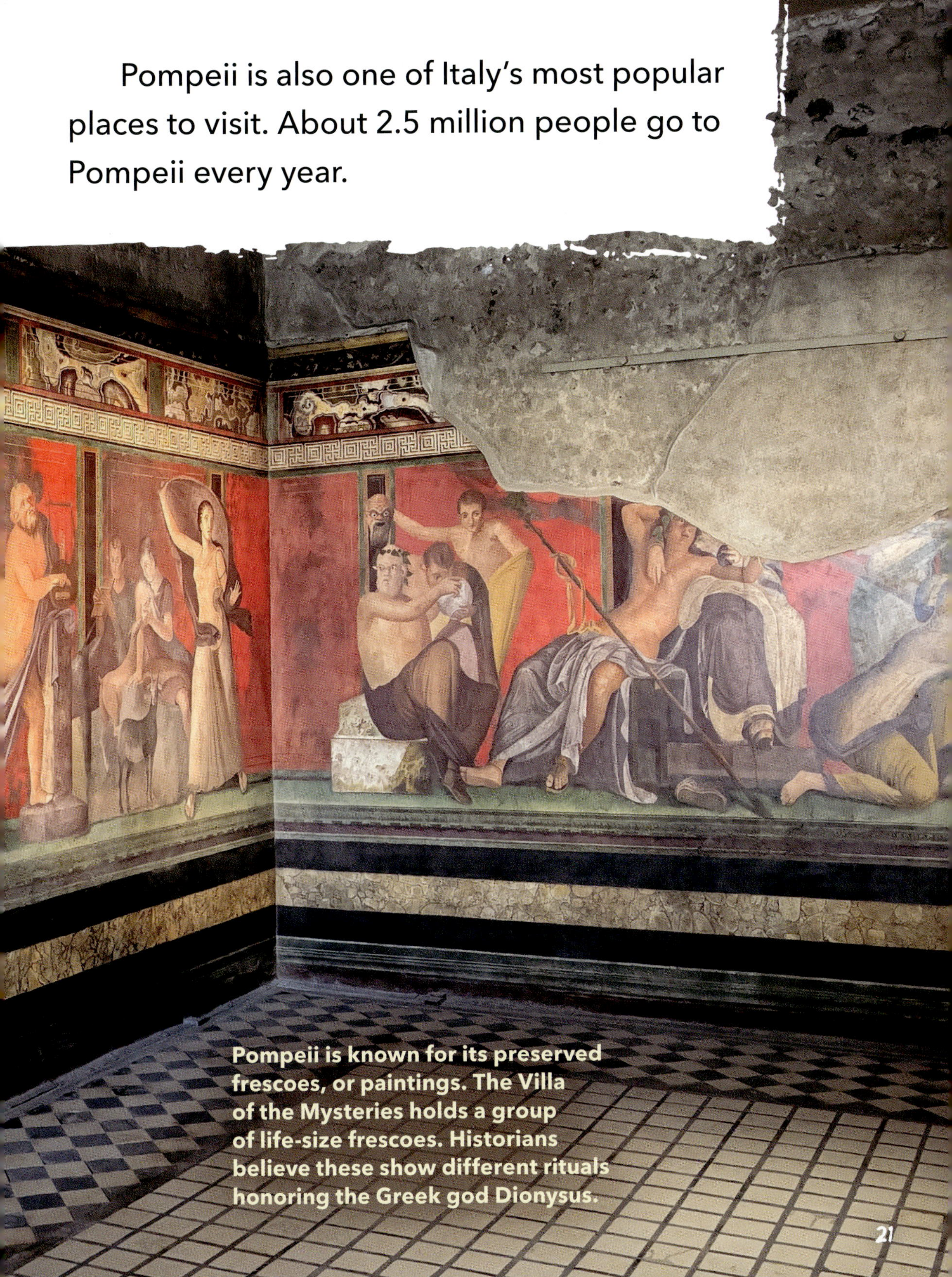

Pompeii is known for its preserved frescoes, or paintings. The Villa of the Mysteries holds a group of life-size frescoes. Historians believe these show different rituals honoring the Greek god Dionysus.

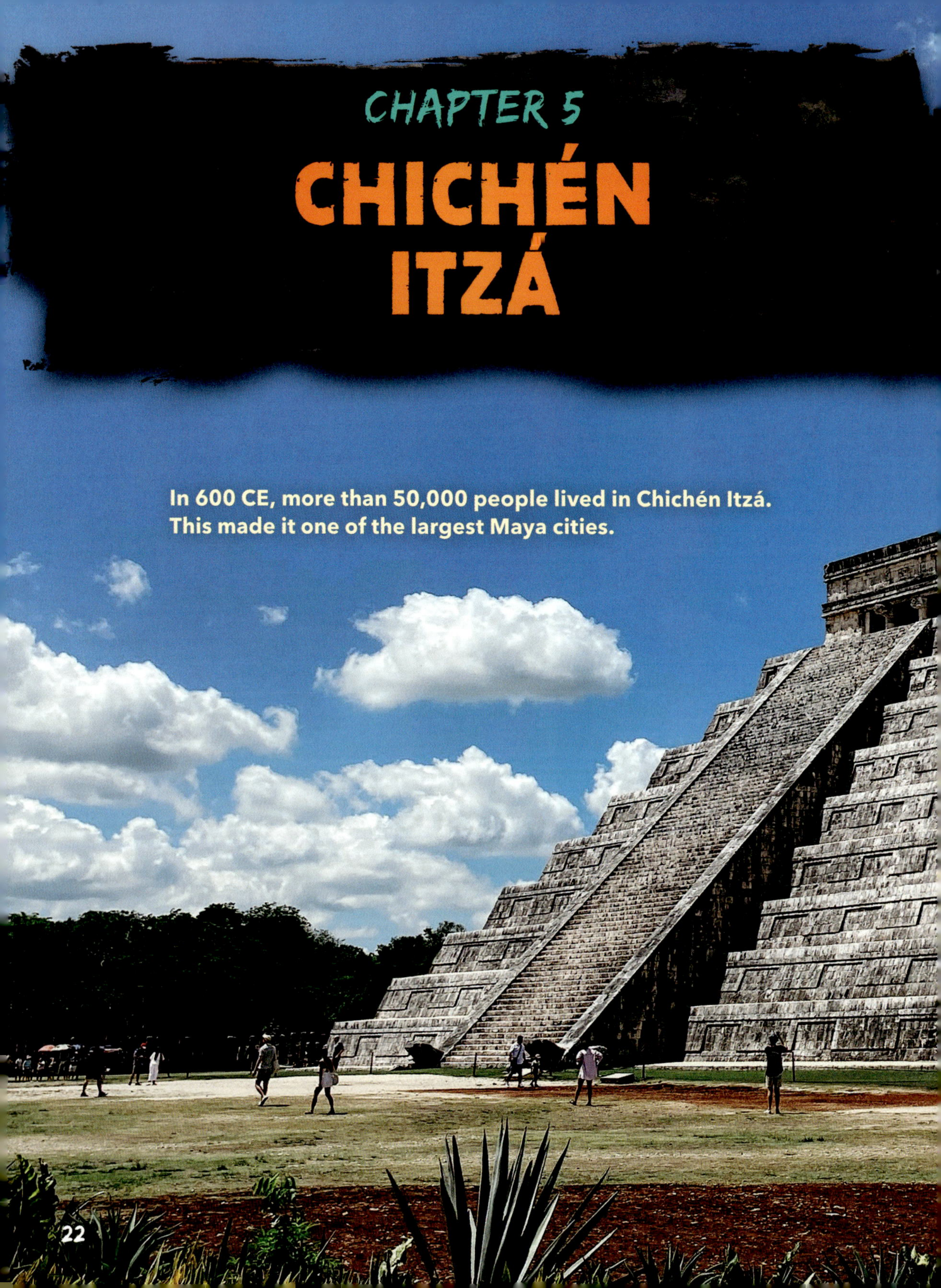

## CHAPTER 5

# CHICHÉN ITZÁ

In 600 CE, more than 50,000 people lived in Chichén Itzá. This made it one of the largest Maya cities.

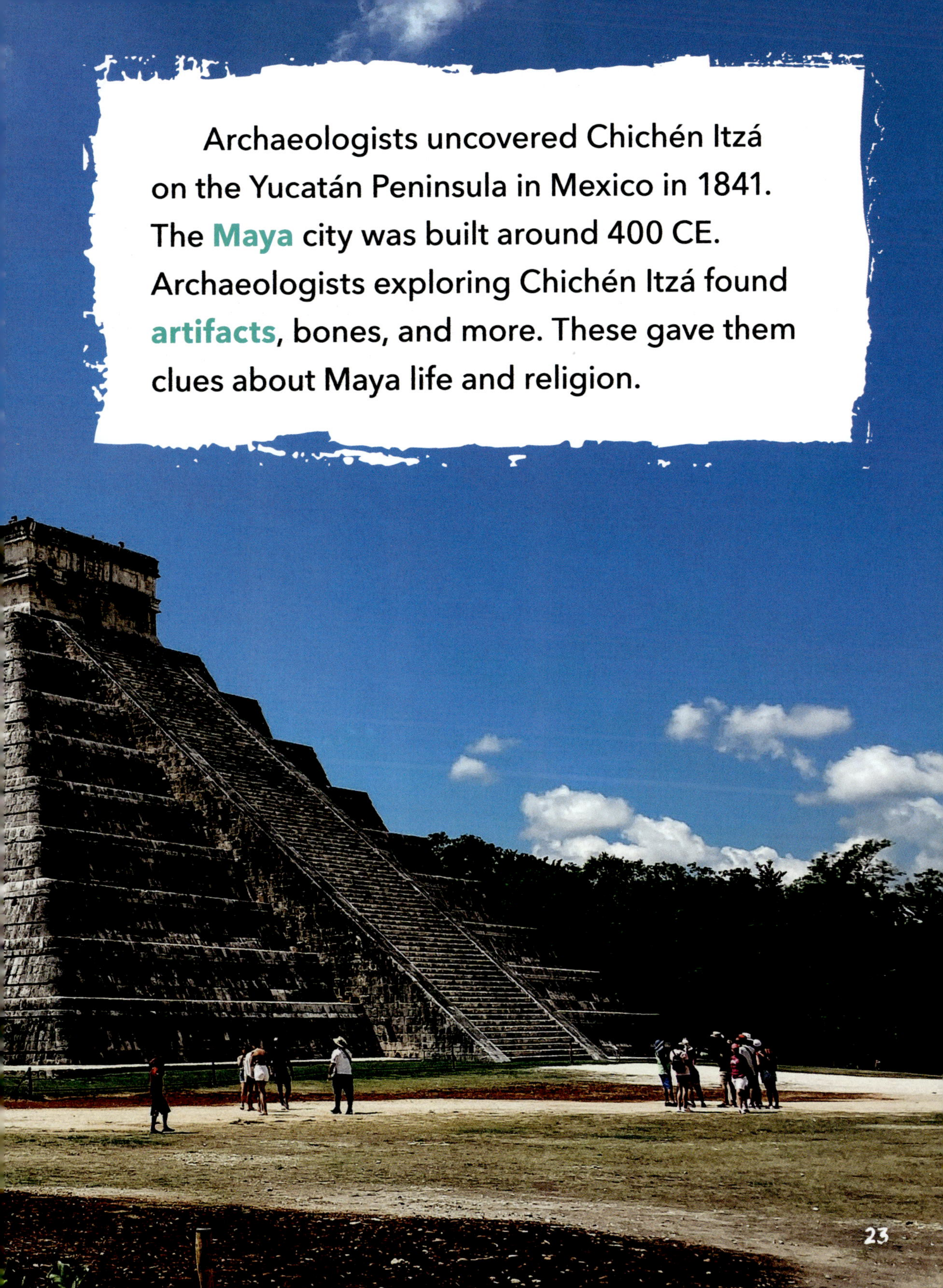

Archaeologists uncovered Chichén Itzá on the Yucatán Peninsula in Mexico in 1841. The **Maya** city was built around 400 CE. Archaeologists exploring Chichén Itzá found **artifacts**, bones, and more. These gave them clues about Maya life and religion.

The **Maya** built Chichén Itzá around **cenotes**. These were very sacred to the Maya. They believed the cenotes connected them to the gods. The Maya threw many offerings into the cenotes.

Archaeologists found gold, pottery, human bones, and more in the cenotes. They think these offerings were for the rain god, Chaac.

The Sacred Cenote is also known as the sacred well. It is 200 feet (61 m) wide and held more than 200 offerings.

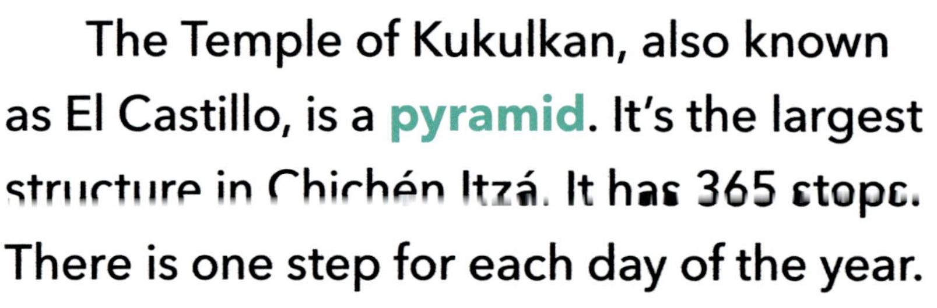

The Temple of Kukulkan, also known as El Castillo, is a **pyramid**. It's the largest structure in Chichén Itzá. It has 365 steps. There is one step for each day of the year.

During certain times of the year, the sunset creates shadows on the sides of the stairs. These shadows look like Kukulkan, the feathered snake god. The **Maya** believed Kukulkan represented creation and rebirth.

### XTREME FACT

**Clapping in front of the stairs creates an interesting sound. Some people think it sounds like a quetzal bird. The Maya believed this sacred bird represented light, goodness, freedom, and wealth.**

The shadows on the stairs are known as the descent of Kukulkan. This only happens twice a year during a celestial event known as the equinox.

Archaeologists have recently found multiple secret tunnels under Chichén Itzá. They think these lead to a hidden **cenote** under the Temple of Kukulkan. The tunnels can help archaeologists unlock more mysteries about the **Maya**.

There are around 7,000 cenotes in the Yucatán Peninsula. Many of them have not been explored. But some of them are open to the public.

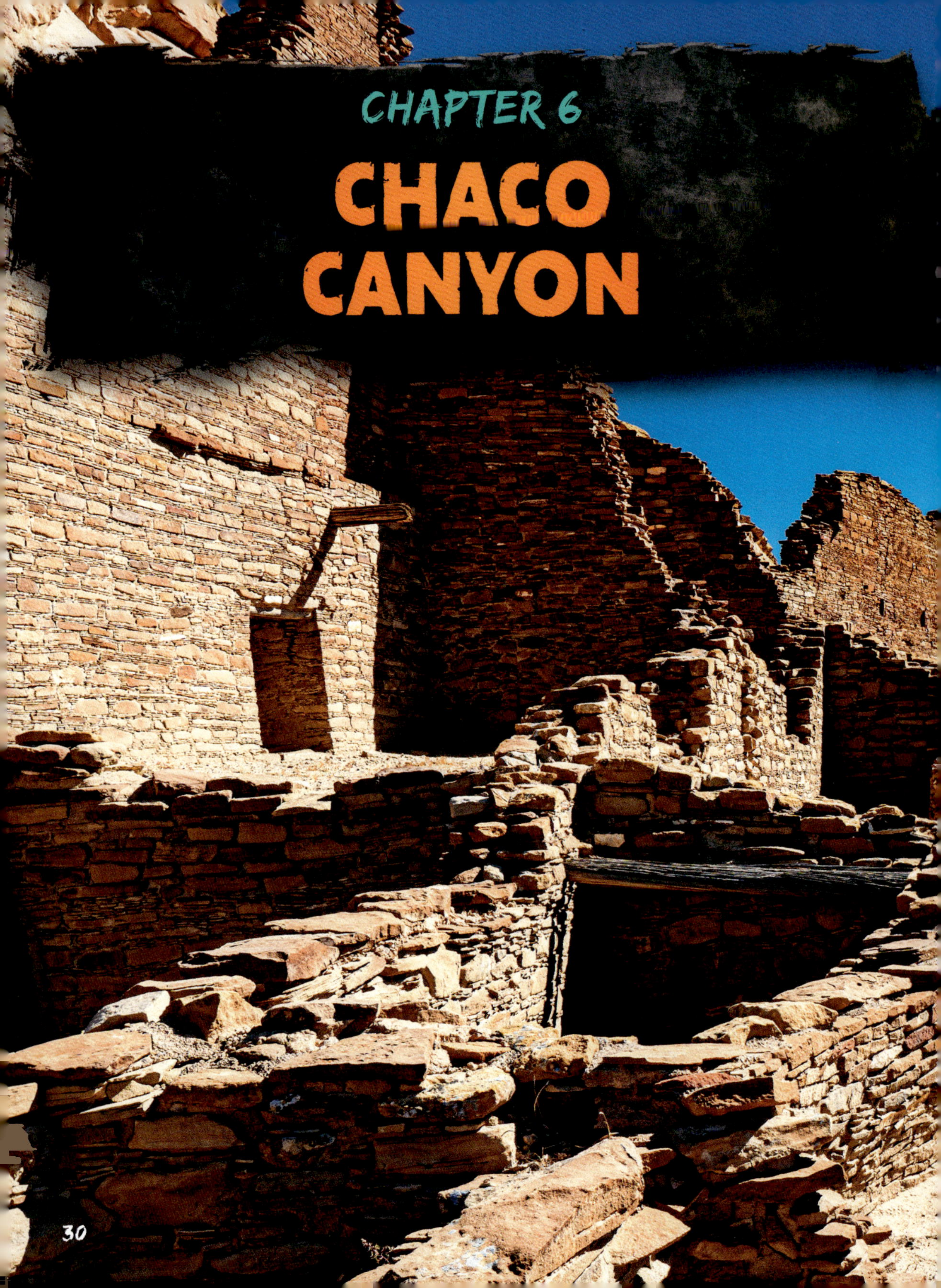

CHAPTER 6

# CHACO CANYON

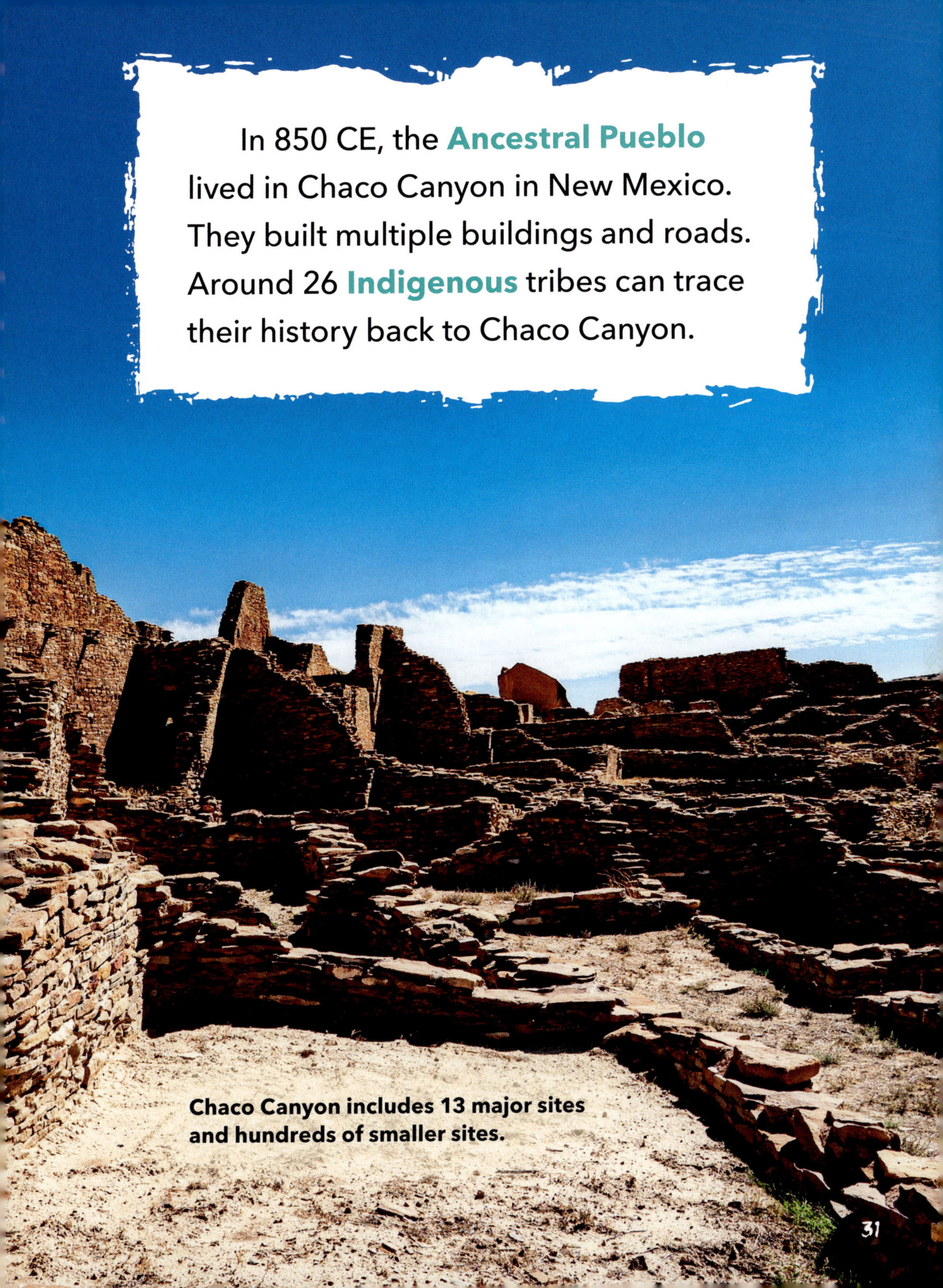

In 850 CE, the **Ancestral Pueblo** lived in Chaco Canyon in New Mexico. They built multiple buildings and roads. Around 26 **Indigenous** tribes can trace their history back to Chaco Canyon.

**Chaco Canyon includes 13 major sites and hundreds of smaller sites.**

The **Ancestral Pueblo** built great houses. These include Pueblo Bonito, Una Vida, and more. Archaeologists noticed that the houses were carefully placed. They line up with the sun, moon, and **cardinal directions**. This means the Ancestral Pueblo planned where to build. It also means they studied engineering and astronomy.

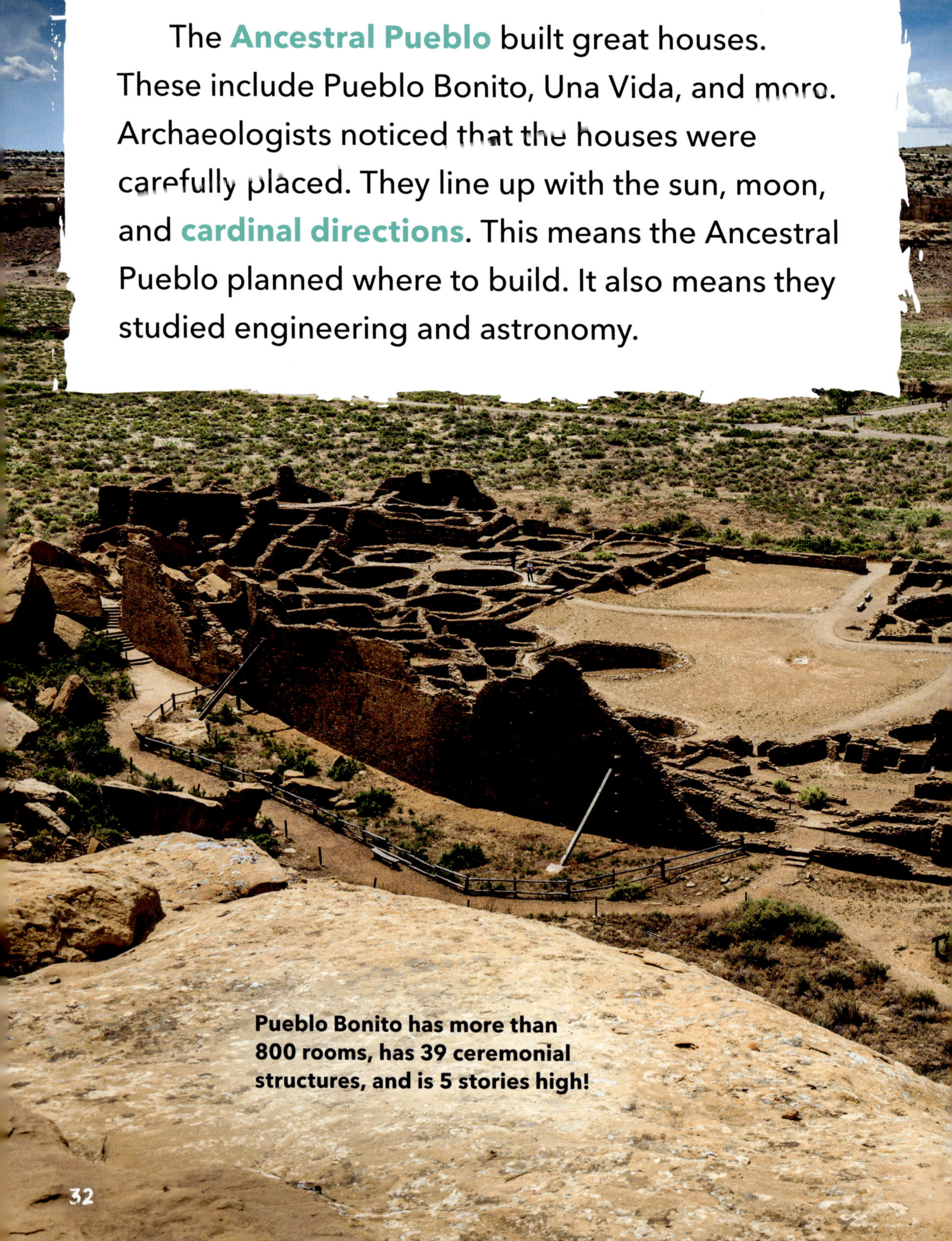

**Pueblo Bonito has more than 800 rooms, has 39 ceremonial structures, and is 5 stories high!**

## XTREME FACT

Archaeologists found petroglyphs, or ancient rock carvings, in Chaco Canyon. They also found pictographs, which are ancient paintings or writings.

For more than 100 years, archaeologists explored Chaco Canyon. They studied the buildings, roads, and **artifacts**. These helped them learn about the **Ancestral Pueblo**. Archaeologists uncovered tools such as fire starters, needles, and more. They also found blankets made of animal fur and turkey feathers.

**XTREME FACT**

A small **Ancestral Pueblo** blanket can include more than 11,000 turkey feathers!

The Ancestral Pueblo used petroglyphs (*pictured*) and pictographs to communicate with each other.

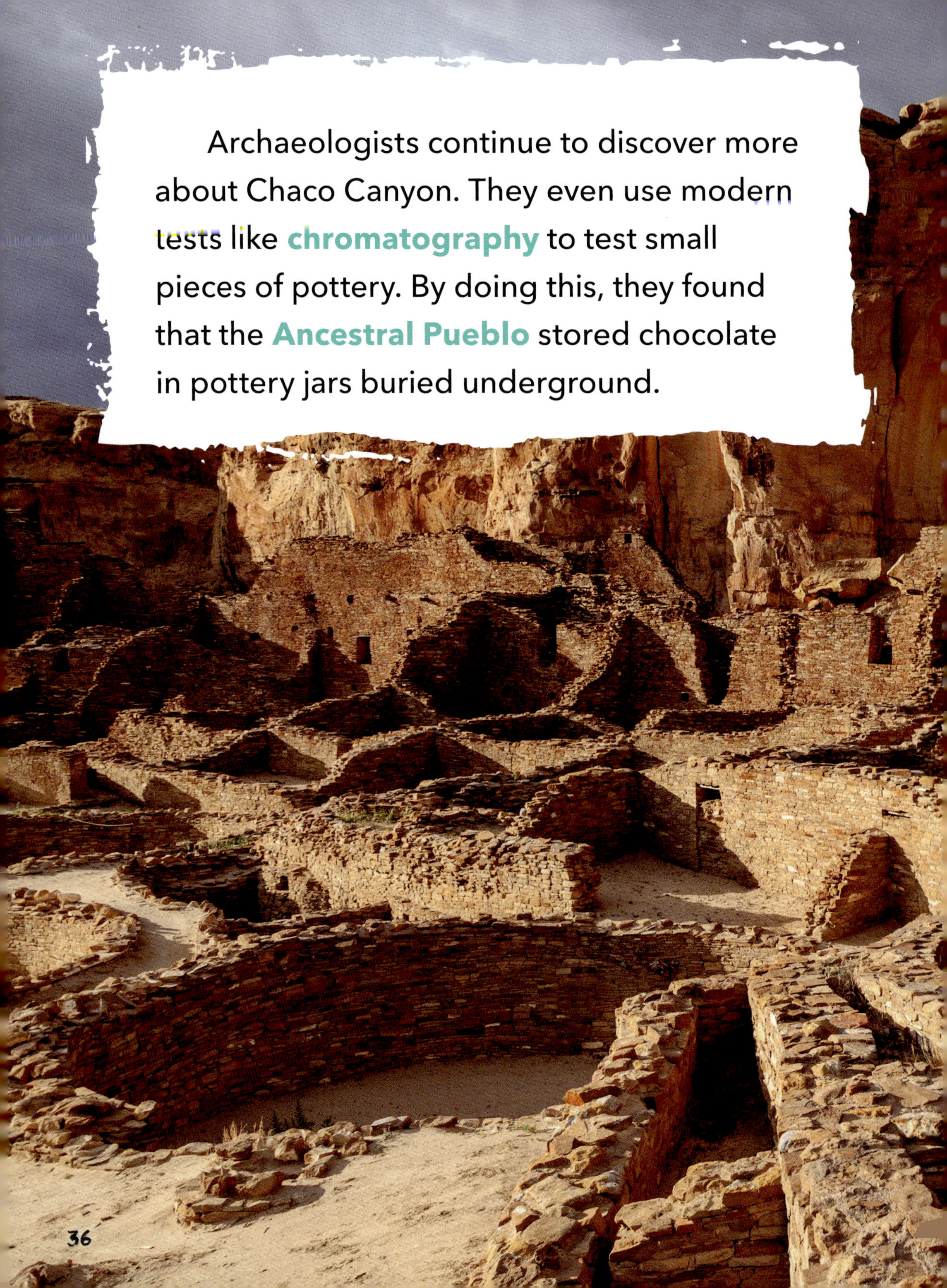

Archaeologists continue to discover more about Chaco Canyon. They even use modern tests like **chromatography** to test small pieces of pottery. By doing this, they found that the **Ancestral Pueblo** stored chocolate in pottery jars buried underground.

Chaco Canyon is a cultural and spiritual center for Indigenous peoples. Indigenous people and park rangers offer tours, educational programs, and other events for visitors.

CHAPTER 7

# SERPENT MOUND

The Serpent Mound is 1,376 feet (419 m) long.

The Serpent Mound in Ohio is a mystery. Scientists know that ancient **Indigenous** people stacked layers of earth and clay into a snake shape. But they don't know why. Many wonder if it honors the stars or is a calendar.

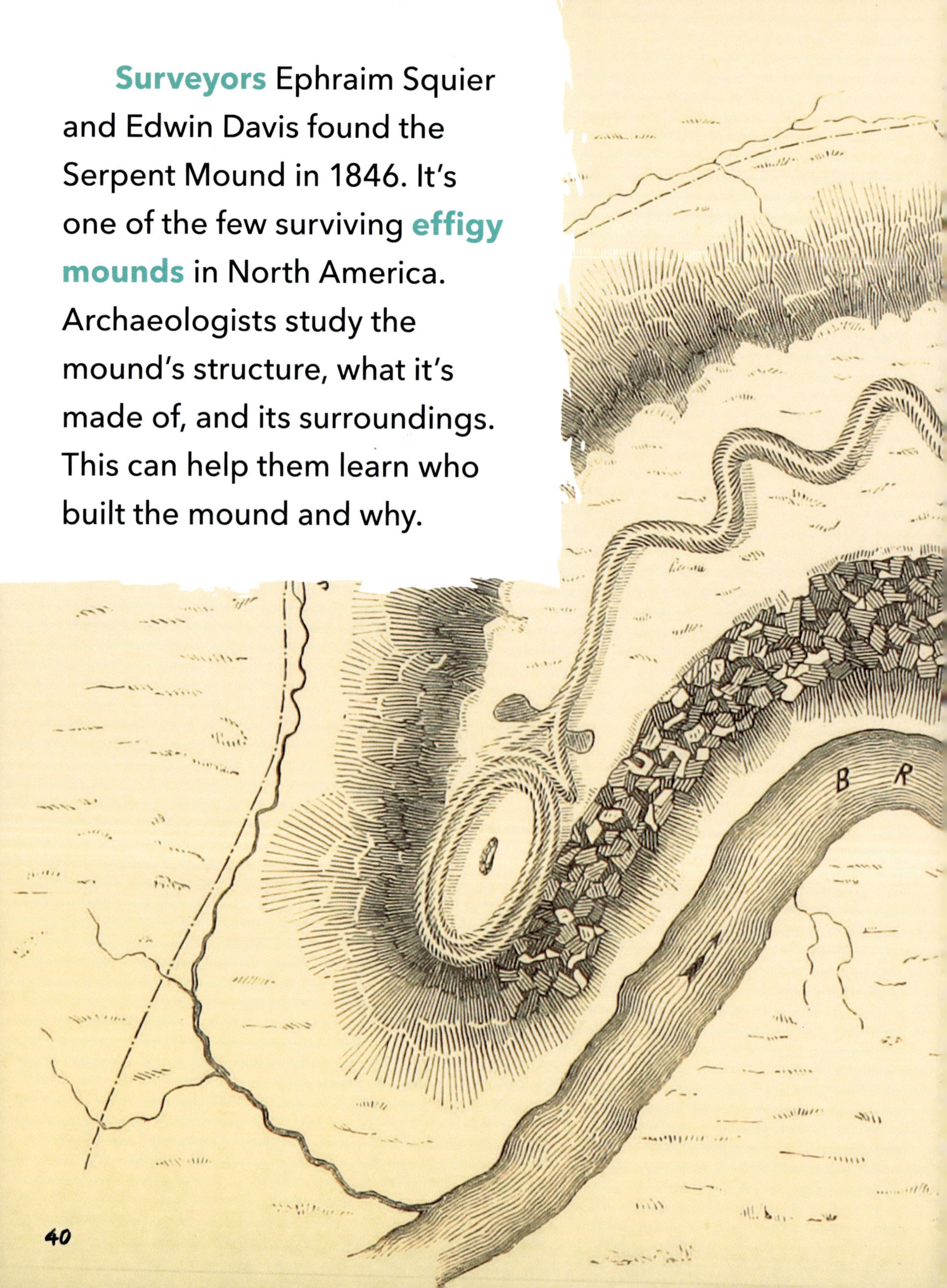


**Surveyors** Ephraim Squier and Edwin Davis found the Serpent Mound in 1846. It's one of the few surviving **effigy mounds** in North America. Archaeologists study the mound's structure, what it's made of, and its surroundings. This can help them learn who built the mound and why.

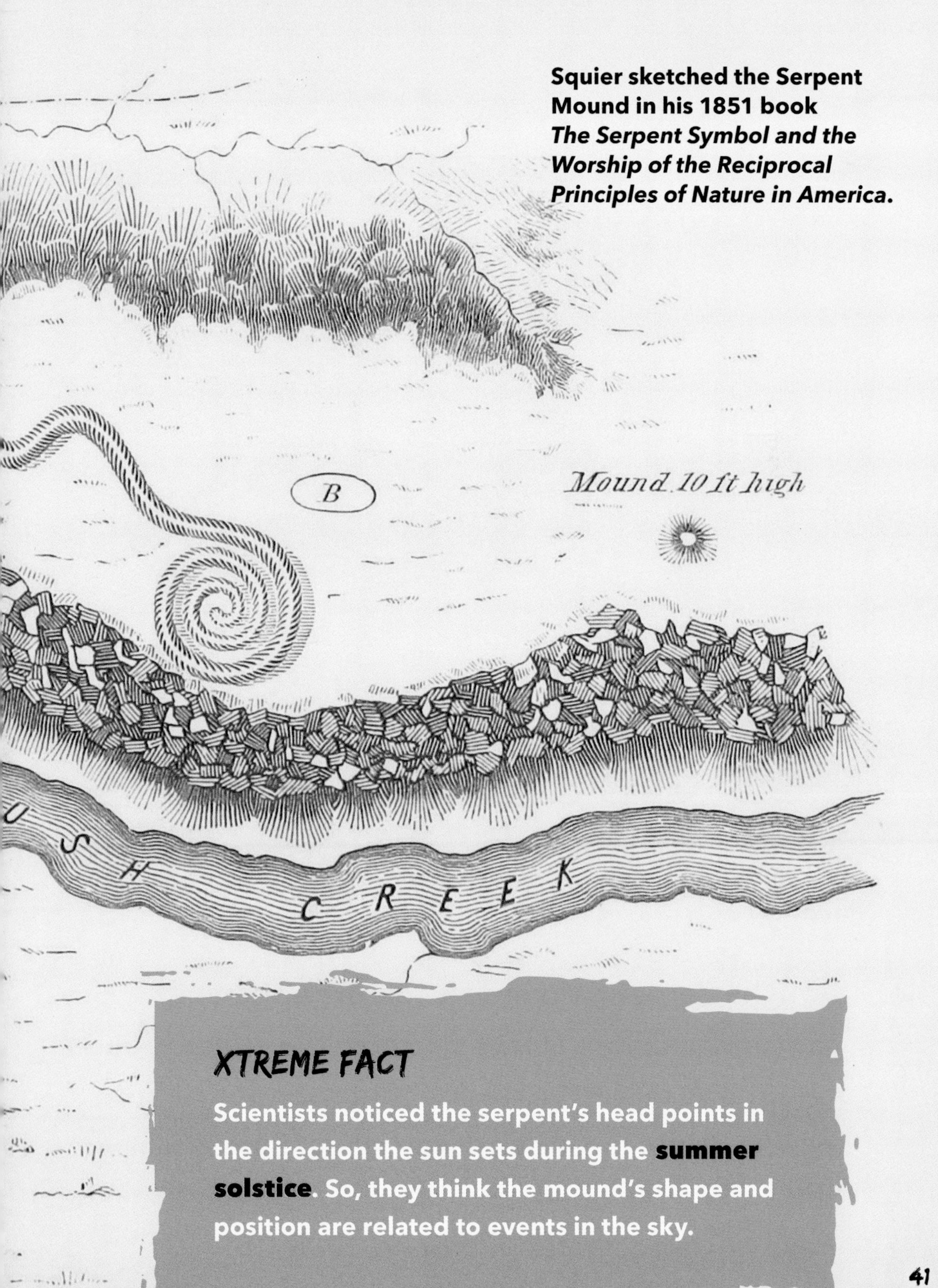


Squier sketched the Serpent Mound in his 1851 book *The Serpent Symbol and the Worship of the Reciprocal Principles of Nature in America.*

## XTREME FACT

Scientists noticed the serpent's head points in the direction the sun sets during the **summer solstice**. So, they think the mound's shape and position are related to events in the sky.

The Serpent Mound sits on the edge of a **meteorite** crater. Scientists know the crater formed about 330 million years ago. But they don't know exactly when the mound was made. Some believe the **Adena** built it around 320 BCE. Others think the **Fort Ancient** created it around 1000 CE.

The Serpent Mound is a protected archaeological site and a National Historic Landmark.

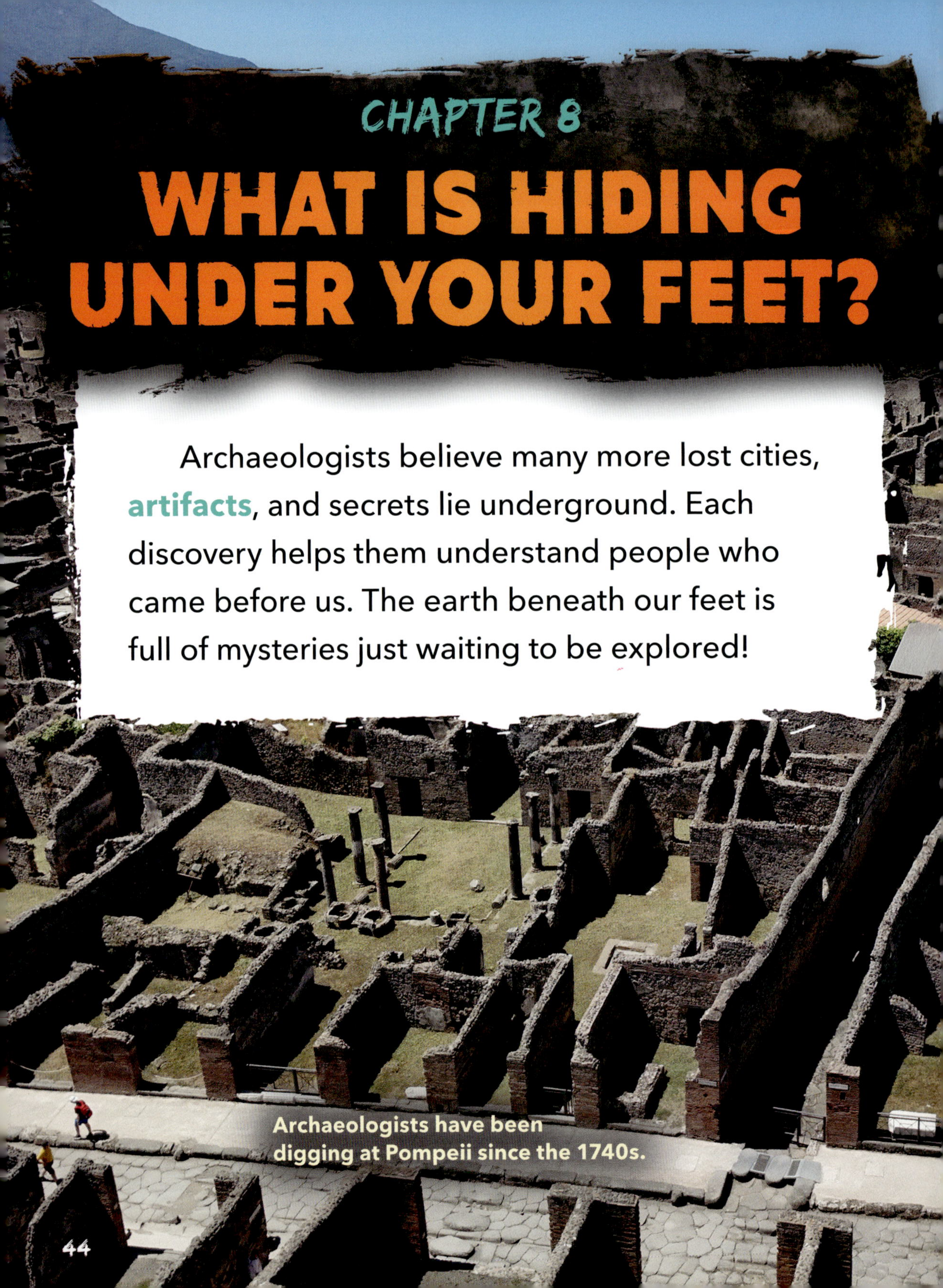

CHAPTER 8

# WHAT IS HIDING UNDER YOUR FEET?

Archaeologists believe many more lost cities, **artifacts**, and secrets lie underground. Each discovery helps them understand people who came before us. The earth beneath our feet is full of mysteries just waiting to be explored!

Archaeologists have been digging at Pompeii since the 1740s.

# XTREME CHALLENGE

**TAKE THE QUIZ BELOW AND PUT WHAT YOU'VE LEARNED TO THE TEST!**

1) If you discovered an ancient city, what artifacts would you look for?

2) Why do you think archaeologists search for ancient sites?

3) Why is it important to protect and preserve ancient sites?

4) What happened to the people who lived in Pompeii?

# GLOSSARY

**Adena**–an ancient Indigenous people who lived in the Ohio Valley from around 500 BCE to 100 CE.

**Ancestral Pueblo**–an ancient Indigenous people who lived in modern-day Arizona, New Mexico, Colorado, and Utah from around 100 CE to 1600 CE.

**artifact**–an object made by humans long ago for a practical purpose.

**cardinal directions**–the four main points on a compass: north, south, east, and west.

**cenote**–a large, deep hole in the ground that is filled with water.

**chromatography**–a scientific process where different parts of a mixture are separated using a gas or liquid. Scientists use this process to identify the different chemicals in a mixture.

**effigy mound**–a hill or pile of earth, usually in the shape of an animal, made by people long ago, possibly for burials and ceremonies.

**Fort Ancient**–an ancient Indigenous people who lived along the Ohio River from about 1000 BCE to 1700 CE.

**historian**–a person who studies or writes about past events.

**Indigenous**–native to a certain place.

**jewelry**–pretty things that are worn for decoration.

**Maya**–an ancient Indigenous people who lived in Central America and Mexico from about 250 CE to 900 CE.

**meteorite**–a space object that hits the surface of the earth.

**pyramid**—a large ancient structure with a square base and four triangle walls that meet at the top.

**summer solstice**—a day when the sun is at its highest point in the sky, marking the longest day of the year.

**surveyor**—a person who measures a piece of land to determine its shape, area, and boundaries.

**thermopolium**—an ancient Roman food shop. Thermopolia are multiple ancient Roman food shops.

**United Nations**—a group of nations formed in 1945. Its goals are peace, human rights, security, and social and economic development.

**volcano**—a deep opening in Earth's surface from which hot liquid rock or steam comes out.

# ONLINE RESOURCES

To learn more about archaeological digs, please visit **abdobooklinks.com** or scan this QR code. These links are routinely monitored and updated to provide the most current information available.

# INDEX